# So Late,
# So Soon

Books by Carol Moldaw:

# So Late, So Soon

*New and Selected Poems*

*Carol Moldaw*

ETRUSCAN PRESS
Wilkes University
84 West South Street
Wilkes-Barre, PA 18766
www.etruscanpress.org

Printed in the United States of America

Publisher's Cataloging-in-Publication

CAROL MOLDAW
*So Late, So Soon:*
*New and Selected Poems*
Carol Moldaw 1st ed.
  p. cm.
  Poems.
  ISBN 13: 9780981968728
  ISBN 10: 0981968724

  I. Title.
  PS3563.O392S6 2010        811'.54
                            QBI10-600019

Etruscan Press is committed to sustainability and environmental stewardship. We elected to print this title through Bookmobile on FSC paper that contains 30% post consumer fiber manufactured using biogas energy and 100% wind power.

*for Arthur and Sarah*

# Table of Contents

New Poems

## Quilted Pantoum

Composition is an absolute mystery.
To penetrate the night is one thing
(you get light enough and you levitate),
to be penetrated by the night, another.

To penetrate the night is one thing:
the mind knows what the eye has not seen;
to be penetrated by the night, another.
Overtaken, we feel a certain devotion.

The mind knows what the eye has not seen.
Perfection, of course, cannot be represented.
Overtaken, we feel a certain devotion.
Think of a shibori-dyed silk organza quilt.

Perfection, of course, cannot be represented
pieced and layered, a little bit off the square.
Think of a shibori-dyed silk organza quilt
but without batting, transparent, floating,

pieced and layered, a little bit off the square,
the layers hand-tied together with horsehair
(but without batting, transparent, floating).
Try to understand, court misunderstanding.

The layers hand-tied together with horsehair,
the grids of the layers overlap like voices.
Try to understand, court misunderstanding.
The seams, like leading, show through.

The grids of the layers overlap like voices.
One thing I've got a good grip on is remorse.
The seams, like leading, show through.
Before it's put on paper, it exists in the mind.

One thing I've got a good grip on is remorse.
Technique a hazard, interruptions a disaster,
before it's put on paper, it exists in the mind.
Rectangles lighten the square's weight.

Technique a hazard, interruptions a disaster,
composition is an absolute mystery.
Rectangles lighten the square's weight.
You get light enough and you levitate.

## Ballast

Unmoored, drifting,
I read the urgency I see
in his face as epinephrine-

injected love. I like that
look, and while the moon
wavers, presiding over

my corpus, negotiating
the shrouded terms
of my release, I want

to feel his gravitational,
double-knotted, binding
pull, wrist and waist.

## Narcissi

I like simple flowers best —
the mason jar of daffodils,
tin of mock orange, crock
of purple tulips carried in
the crook of a friend's arm.

I give ornate arrangements
to the nurses, to brighten
their station down the hall,
but the lilies' Lysol stench
infects the whole ward.

While tulips bow to exalt
survival, narcissi coxswain
the skiff of staples rowing
my stomach's fresh fault line
— nothing to do with birth.

Easier, at three, to imagine
bubbling up from nowhere
than from another mother's
tummy. "Can we pretend,"
my daughter asked, sliding

toward me in the tub. Yes,
*if we know we're pretending.*
Now, at six, bringing me
a posterboard get well card,
she takes in my ratty hair,

backless gown, machine-
tethered wrist, oxygen tube
I'm scared to do without,
and keeps to her father's lap
until, sighing like a teenager

giving up her iPod, I bury
my IV, rip out the tube.
*Closer,* I breathlessly coax.
Whoever thought about
croaking? Not now, not me.

## From the Other Side of the World

No wild flowers this year, only wild fires.

The wind in my ears oceanic as I walk home,
louder than the sound of it riffling the grasses.

In my head, the crunch of gravelly sand under my boots,
wind stream, some nursery rhymes, a memory loop:

pacing the length of the hotel room in Guangzhou,
rocking her in my arms, kissing, murmuring, cooing.

At the arroyo's mouth, in the new leaves
of the unburnt cottonwoods, the wind sings even louder.

When I experienced for the first time the storm
of her crying, I knew with a mystic's fierce certainty

that everything I had ever felt, or anything she or I
would ever feel, she had felt already, and so had you,

and I, once, all of it there from the beginning, engulfing us,
our subsequent feelings only riffs on that immensity.

Now, crossing the plank laid across our acequia,
coming to our field, still ringed with the twisted spines

of burnt trees, still strewn with cracked-off branches,
I understand that clarity as a mother, not a mystic,

for it brought with it a task — to ensure that she
could support such intensity and not be consumed.

Under the char, new grass, brighter green than before.

We're always the last in the neighborhood to hear things,
our house set back from the road, our adobe walls thick.

By the time sirens and the acrid smoke woke us,
neighbors were already out in our field, shoring up dirt

and beating back flames with the flats of their shovels.
When Arthur went to join them, I stayed with Sarah.

We've named her *Sarah*. I know you'll never read this —

how could you? You won't come across it, it's not
in your language, which you might not even read, and then

how would you know it was written specifically to you,
not to some other of the thousands of mothers that year

who left a newborn where she could be found,
at the foot of a bridge, in front of an old people's home —

but I'm *impelled* to write you, as though even unread
a missive can transmit — *transmit what?* Assurance

of the well-being of your daughter who is our daughter?
Still a baby in her crib, she hates loud abrupt noises

but slept through the sirens, the frantic shouting, choking
stench. Once or twice, I ran out to gauge the wind-whipped

course of the flames, but from behind our courtyard wall
saw only an eerie orange glow before rushing back in

to check her breathing, the clear ponds of her fringed lids.

You can see that the fire's force created
its own countervailing wind in the s-pattern

of burnt and unburnt grasses, of trees blackened
and toppled near trees standing green. Flushed

from the marsh, two ducks preened, buoyed
on an incinerated tuft. Black spiders scurried

like a living network of exposed nerves
over brittle swaths of ash and untouched pasture,

exhumed debris, flung empties. The convoluted
conception of fate I developed "waiting" for Sarah

had nothing to do with charting or justifying
the coincidence of suffering and good fortune,

it evolved from imagining that what would happen
already had, so that envisioning her in my arms

I could work my way back to when she was
in a particular crib in *x* row of a particular floor

of a certain orphanage and know *that* baby
the one I hold now, thus the one meant to be ours,

since once something has happened it becomes,
de facto, your fate. Like the flicked cigarette

that ignited the marsh; like the marsh itself,
still wet under the cattails' candle stubs.

At my whistle, Raz lifts his nose from snuffling,
trots over, sits for a biscuit, accepts the leash.

A Husky mix, most nights he guards her door.

*A typical Southern beauty,* Arthur's uncle from Beijing
calls her, though about this we know next to nothing:

not whether she was born in the village of your birth,
or whether, pregnant, you traveled south to escape

scrutiny; not whether you were waiting for a son
or already had one. Was her father your husband?

Easy to posit what's beamed across the world,
the country's story, on girls whose own stories

flicker and pulse like the cursive of those fireflies
we chase through unmown fields in early July

before fireworks start, just to feel the buzzing
in our hands. This year, for a week, news crews

with nothing better or worse to cover parked
their satellite dishes in the burnt grass to monitor

the smouldering ashes. Finally, I told them to leave.
*Who are you?* they asked, thinking it pueblo land.

Make peace, I'll tell her, with what you can't know.

For now, love suffices, love eager to suppose
she couldn't be happier with anyone else, even you.

## Vapor Trail

While Mars glints in the sky like a ruby the size
of a grapefruit, like, in a movie, a hand grenade,

lobbed and sizzling, closer to earth now
than what might as well be "ever"— and our daughter,

eight thousand miles from where she was born,
sleeps on the couch the sleep of the safely arrived,

her first great *grand jeté* already behind her —
and, settled next to me, neurons of consciousness

nocturnally slackened, unknotted, in the exalted
sleep of the exhausted, you blow out your cheeks

like a puffer fish afloat in the indigo vat of the vast —
and, though distracted by crickets monotonically

intent on giving me direction from the cracks
and corners, I pursue in lines that don't yet exist

a metaphor's vanishing vapor trail, mushroom
clouds of meaning — a device of the next generation,

handmade, clandestine, intricate, mass produced,
officially sanctioned, beyond my ability to take in,

to ignore, somewhere (it could be anywhere,
if alive we'll read about it with horror) explodes.

## Out of the West

Out of the west, unexpected, lyric,
a stand of yellow irises
rises from the pond muck.

Two horses graze the field,
one limping from the fire they fled.

Matter and spirit meet, love,
*argue,* wherever you rest your eyes,
on microscopic midges, horseflies.

## Matter and Spirit

1. In the Beginning

Mortified by their attraction,
whoever introduced them long forgotten,
Matter and Spirit meet
on the sly,
their affair an open secret.

2.   Upstairs to the Left

Matter turns down the sheets,
Spirit closes the blinds.
An itinerant composer
hearing the creaking bedsprings
fills a page with half-notes,
quarter-notes, melisma.
The desk clerk drowsing
in front of a deck of cards
dreams of palm fronds,
asphalt blistering in the sun.

3.   Together All Night

Whereas Matter
predictably snores,
Spirit can't sleep: even
in the amniotic sac
an insomniac.

4. Rendezvous of One

One day Matter receives a wire:
"indefinite delay — proceed."
So Matter sets off alone,
collects the key, saunters in,
pulls the shade, retreats
to a corner chair, unzips
to filmstrip in his head, footage
shot on the empty bed.

5.   Traffic

Stuck in traffic, Matter
desperately tries telepathy:
*I'll be late, please wait.*
*I'll be late, please wait.*

Spirit gets the message, but
not so above it all after all
turns on her heel,
put out by his feet of clay.

6.   Cat's Cradle

Without Matter, Spirit
knocks about the house,
forgets to dress.

Hours evaporate
without having come
full boil, the day

a sketchpad
blank of the rough
thoughts one had

thought to but didn't
sketch out. Hands
ache with inaction,

if only to mold clay,
string a cat's
cradle, cradle a cat.

7. Chain Reaction

The bliss that Spirit feels,
the satisfaction that is Matter's,
as they commingle, are they,

do they look, the same?
A full moon's held note,
a chain of clouds like a chain

of islands, the unfurling fern
frond of a seahorse's tail,
a Siberian iris, a cool blue ibis,

rain inside a mausoleum, rain
under a tin roof, a porcupine
and a spice pomander — paired,

what is there to bind them?
Aside from a wandering
mind's bliss, its satisfaction.

## Still Life

*for my mother*

In foothills where wisps
of cloud are sometimes
trapped like sheep's wool

caught on brambles,
her mind wanders. The fog
stretches like an endless

chain of paper dolls,
not impenetrable, but lacy—
doilies of fog that dissolve

into singular drops of dew
and leave her cheek, even
after all the years, soft

and globed as petals:
a rose in her own
cutting bed, companion

to spindly larkspurs,
pin-wheeled zinnias,
ranunculi shy as koi,

all bred to fill shelves
of gleaming vases:
little capless alembics

for buds, low centerpieces
guests can see across,
majestic flared rectangles

that, reflected in the mirror
above the mantle, reveal
the arrangements' backs.

On one couch, she gazes
at lilies all morning
every day for a week

while the petals brown
and detach. On another,
like a solitary navigator

mesmerized by stars,
out the south-facing
bay window she fixes

on a Japanese maple
leaf's five points, but
by the time she plants

stockinged feet on sisal,
her mind is scoured,
transparent, already

reaching for the cut
stems in the sink,
still to be arranged.

## Premonition

Each book short a poem,
the poem I couldn't yet write.
My father exits; thinking
he is going outside I open
the door to follow, find

him naked on the other side
facing me unshielded, vulnerable
to the rise in my voice.
The poem I can't yet write
saves for itself a blank page

for when it can't be avoided,
a promissory note come due.
For now, the account still
running, the line of credit
open, the debt not yet settled.

## Torn Silk

*for Janis  (1958–2005)*

*Pearls set in bird bone*
*Ashes kneaded into clay*
*The sound of tearing silk*
*A dog trotting away*

> We used to idle on the washed-out riverbed's
> palimpsest of the river's drifting course,
> tossing sticks against the current for Raz,
> bemoaning in the same breath a mislaid earring
> and a misleading man, swapping prophetic dreams
> like raw gems sifted from the silt of sleep . . .

*Ashes kneaded into clay*
*Stamped with a double wheel*
*A dog trotting away*
*The wind in a sudden whirl*

> . . . but never suspected the stealth bomb
> about to balloon in Bruce's brain, your shared life
> collapsing in the ruin of a synapse. When you lit
> death's acetylene torch, once and for all
> burning off dross of need, sheen of strength,
> your new boyfriend heard the shot but thought
> the stack of pots and pans that you had washed
> had fallen off the overladen dish rack
> and to avoid another fight spent the day hiking.

*Stamped with a double wheel*
*To help you on your way*
*The wind in a sudden whirl*
*A basket's coiled weave*

    The shot went clean through, leaving
    your beauty so intact, when Kimi came by
    she thought you were sleeping off a bender
    or some sleeping pills, until a line of blood
    in the crack of your mouth led to a red pillow
    under your fanned hair, and then the tacky feel
    of blood her own shoes tracked everywhere.

*To help you on your way*
*Pearls set in bird bone*
*A basket's coiled weave*
*The sound of tearing silk*

## Bone Soup

Three years, still dead
but alive inside me:
in a dream, talking to him
on the phone, spooning
soup from his bones.

## Canning in Chimayo
### for Emily

"Feed me fuck me feed me fuck me feed me"—
knife a whirligig, each trochee slashed off,

translucent venous beet wheels heaped
like raked-in poker chips, her disquisition

on canning upended by the nightly crapshoot
she can't in her viscera shake, only vitiate

at the chopping block. Eyes pop. Widen.
Not one of us can slice that fast. Someone

passes a jay. Someone pours more wine.
Cheeks streaked, wrists ribboned, thumbs

pressed to temples, she aprons her head.
Then the beets are vinegared, the whole mess

sealed in mason jars; the Italian plums
eviscerated, mounded with sugar, put to boil;

the corn cobs flayed, pearl onion and red
pepper strips stirred into the kernels, all

four of us at the counter, mulling it over:
*feed me, fuck me,* pressure cooker, preserves.

## October Sunrise

Here, on the western edge of the time zone,
I sleep in, but it's dark when I get up.
On the other side of the divide, you rise
at the same moment: though it's early, light
already pastels and recontours the sky.
Ahead of me, the day, a nickle buffalo,
flared nostrils and scuffed up dust clouds
through which I dimly see you gather Sarah
and start the car, the cold engine steaming
my drained cup. A pen lies on the desk,
a tool in a dentist's tray, its gleam patent,
prying. *Open your mouth*, it wheedles, *open
wide*. Twisting away, I glimpse two chairs
askew, crushed napkins, your untouched tea.

## The Light Out Here
### for Arthur

Looking up "taxidermy" this morning
in the same edition of the American Heritage
that you gave me, I saw a word
bracketed and asterisked in bright red ink,
something neither of us would do —

not even with a light pencil.
I bet whoever marked up "taphonomy"
had been rummaging in Moonlight Gems,
where browsing last week I found
a fossilized shark tooth for Sarah.

Remember the pair of hummingbirds
she discovered on the screened porch?
— Iridescent, green-gorgetted; the female
crushed under an overturned tin tub,
the male with one perfect wing laid out

as if awaiting its Dürer. "Black-chinned,
not Calliope," you said, correcting me
as you passed the field guide. "I'm sure
we'll both put them in poems." But mine
languished, quarantined in a quatrain.

*A bird can be as many different birds,*
I tell myself, *as it has observers,*
and writers, like prospectors, often stake
claims in the most crowded streams,
but stationed here, I scrupulously avoid

rhapsodizing the clear golden light,
the freight trains' haunted baritone,
instead combing old notebooks
for neglected data, the severed deer head
we stumbled on last fall, the fire

five years ago that cut an s-pattern
through our field, leaving tufts of grass
untouched amid wide swaths of char.
Unused or overused, an image can ossify,
you have to test it — take the javelinas

yesterday, in a curiosity shop window,
fronting a display case of black sombreros.
Two of them, as if trotting in place,
each on its own rock slab, one
not very convincingly baring its fangs.

*— Marfa, Texas*

## Every Which Way

Sometimes you feel
him inside you

when he is
not there, sometimes

when he is
distracted you don't.

Toes bent back
sometimes wayward

on calves, breath
to accelerating breath

agape, sometimes
there is no *you* or *he*

only exothermic bursts
looping the closed

matchless circuit,
your reconfigured selves.

## So Late, So Soon

Don't assume the car
ahead is headed where
you want to go. Don't

mindlessly follow it.
Pass the farmstand,
graveyard, kennel,

low-to-the-ground
stone-carved clover,
your mark. Take

a sharp left. Where
light scrolls a sycamore,
incising its bark and

leaves, pull over, let
yourself be bedazzled
until the light scoots.

You'll see a dirt road
with no hedge. Turn
right and keep going

East, toward the spit
wherein you think
your destination lies.

Go farther than you
imagined, until the road
straightens, narrows.

If you find yourself
in a mounting reverie
regarding the eloquent

slope of his shoulder,
the sweetly sustained
ardor of his inquiry,

the way he heaps bliss
upon you, then spoons
you to sleep — again,

pull over. Compose
yourself by scribbling
a note to be e-mailed

later. And if, by now,
tired of admiring day
lilies, buttercups,

*you just want to be there,*
check for speed traps
before accelerating.

Soon, on your right,
you'll come to cow
pasture, rolling field,

silo, barns, stacked
hay, and then a sudden
shadow — the woods:

always the woods before
your arrival; a clearing;
the unanticipated bay.

*from* Taken
from
the
River

## 64 Panoramic Way

Like easy conversation,
rambling, obliquely angled,
the winding street traverses
the steep residential hill.

Stone stairs ladder-stitch
the street's tiers; every few
rungs open on terraces,
windows glinting through hedges,

sunlight feathering grass.
At the first switchback,
pine needles tufted with dog fur
pad the wide cracked steps

leading to a cottage and two
ramshackle shingle houses.
From the lintel of an illegal
basement apartment, magenta

fuchsia, silent bells,
bob and sag over a pot's rim.
Higher, up wooden stairs
built over rubble, we climb

to the top deck. What was
our garden now grows wild
onions' white flowers,
and butter-yellow weeds —

winter's mohair throw
draping a bare mattress.
By late spring someone else
or no one will be bending

to pick cool herbs
like single guitar notes.
Something knots my throat.
Indecipherable

decibels begin jackhammering
inside #D — our old address.
Black Sabbath? Iron Maiden?
I know our own records

by the first chord. Pounding,
we try the unlocked door
and pick our way through
a year's domestic fallout:

dropped clothes, album sleeves,
mattresses blocking entrances,
plates, cups, hangers, books.
I trip trying not to look.

Waving on the balcony,
an old guest, now our host,
offers us the view.
At this time of year,

no yellow beach roses
tumble the latticed railing,
no draft of honeysuckle,
no bees flitting near their hive.

Cars nose around the hairpin turn.
Looking past Berkeley's hazy
flat grids, past Oakland,
you can see, as if you've flicked

a painted fan open, a striped
spinnaker tacking the wide bay,
three bridges, and San Francisco
shrugging off her damp negligee.

## Stanford Hills

Tiptoe on a sturdy branch,
taller than the tallest girl,
she reaches into the sky

and pulls at a tangled thread.
Rows of clouds unpurl.
She can see miles ahead,

she can almost see Webb Ranch
across the tawny hills,
its silos, horse barns, fields,

and the two rickety shacks
where they buy vegetables
from Mexican women whose men

bending over harvest fields
fill giant burlap sacks.
She'd like to have a sack

to wear for Halloween.
She'd sew beads on the hem
and be an Indian maiden.

Bright feathers down her back!
Last year as Fairy Queen
in a tinsel diadem

she waved her foil wand
and charmed the cul-de-sac.
Now she jumps, rolling beyond

cowflops, ants, a scraped shin;
flattened fields of rye;
her mother calling her in.

## Patrilineage

The uncle's lopped-off head,
Cossacks in the sister's bed,
and the boy who hid, then fled,
took a name from the river
and crossed the sea, found
Ida, had you—who had me.

## The Sorceress

Practitioner
of the most deliberate
arts, deflector
of spirits, interceptor

of wills, I toss
boys off course
for one night, one day,
an hour's hallucinatory

pleasures. Other women
use their charm to keep
their men; I use men
to keep my charms. Magic

thrives on man's embrace,
overarches earthly
inspiration to cascade
into one glorious vortex,

pool of all my best concoctions.

## Menses

Yesterday, a thread
of blood, a spool
unwinding; homespun
nubbed yarn, red
saturated strands I
wound round my finger;
moon-cloth, harbinger
of no one, unwoven.

Juice of the crushed
pomegranate seed,
disintegrated nest,
floating egg freed,
dam burst and flushed
clean in the spring
tide's flux; slowly
draining watery breast.

Taboo to discuss,
ochre we daub and smear,
a lunar calendar's
primary ink: thirteen
ruby moons a year
flowing from luscious hips
flower on soft lips,
poppy, rose, hibiscus.

## The Wood Spirit Speaks

Your friend heard my mute song's
thin stream on the hiker's path
and knelt. Whorled and knotted,
charred, arching, furled
like a wave, sinuous as smoke,
I fit her grasp—a hook.
Now you have me, *your genie,*
and my song sticks in your throat.

A five-inch wisp of wood,
propped on your desk three years
while you pieced together scraps
of repeatedly x'd-out words
describing how the hole
bored clean through my left eye
and the right's curved lid-line
make me seem half asleep

and half haunted, a skull.
I don't want to wait anymore.
My goat-mouth, a crosshatched,
nicked slit, is always open,
my windpipe's air hole exposed
above its tongue-flap,
a foreshortened arm flung wide
while, chanteuse, I hold my note.

Writing these words I've put
in your mind to put in my mouth,
certain no one will see
what you see, daunted, you drop
your pen in despair and pull
from the drawer a strip of black
Egyptian cotton cloth
to bind and muzzle me.

I only pray it's days,
hours, not weeks and months,
till you have heart enough
to take me up again—
though not one splintered strand
of my ram's horn headdress,
my two high-piled topknots,
will meanwhile whiten or uncoil.

# From Assisi
### for J.O.

1.

Candles at vespers
and blazing torches;
booms; lulls; whispers;
alternating bells;
far and near churches.

2.

Like a rose window,
the round moon rose
above the basilica.
What face did she show
to him, in Africa?

3.

Medieval, thus urban —
archways and alleys
plastered with comets;
the straw magi's
fluttering turbans.

4.

Awakened, lovesick,
to tribal drumming
in my Umbrian attic.
Clear synchronicity —
and then more static.

5.
A beveled mirror,
a vanity for a desk;
books halving the bed;
fog, dawn and dusk;
figs, oranges, bread.

6.
An unfinished Flight
in a hillside chapel,
hidden from sunlight
behind a bare altar,
near Eve and her apple.

7.
Following sheeptracks,
taking turns at the helm
of Melina's carriage,
talking of home,
art, poetry, marriage.

8.
Doves flocking for seed
flung from a satchel
every day at noon
beside Minerva's Temple
in the Piazza Commune.

9.
Studying frescoes
of Francis preaching
to the attentive birds;
casting the *I Ching,*
weighing its words.

10.
Squeaking bicycles,
housemaids' quarrels,
wheelbarrows, a rooster,
sheep and church bells,
heard from my cloister.

## At Deathbed

When your father died
his hair was blown
all to one side
and his mouth kept
the shape of his breath.
It too looked windswept,
oval, not round.
The lack of sound
when his breath stopped
was itself a prayer
absorbed by the air.
A gentle death.
He was light as a seed.
While he labored to breathe
you stroked his arm
and searched his eyes.
He held your gaze
as though, now freed
from human ties,
he could look at you
from closer at hand
and not risk harm.
All that was left
in his eyes was love.
They were clear blue
cornflowers faded
the color of stars.
Before they were closed
his chill gaunt face
once so bereft
was swept with grace.

## The Window Box

Packets of seeds, lobelia, cosmos, and phlox,
meant for a bedroom's redwood window box,

seven years, two states, three apartments back,
still rubberbanded, a neat rattling stack

stashed under paperclips in my desk drawer.
I remember going to the garden store,

its greenhouse windows fogged with thick moist air,
the hanging ferns, the delicate maidenhair,

big water-stained clay pots, rustling bamboo,
bird baths, broad-fanned palms, a cherub statue,

the yellow hoses coiled to strike like snakes,
the shovels, pitchforks, hoes, and gangly rakes.

Late afternoon southwestern light would splash
that bedroom window and bounce against the sash,

dappling the leaves and air before it fell.
Some days a few drops leaking in would swell —

light absorbing light in shallow pools
that slowly sank into the floor. Time fools

with things, but how light changes stays the same
year to year: the August sun that came

to fill our window box with cardamom light
must be lengthening on the ledge, though here it's night

and the full moon gapes behind her billowing curtain,
her face half-hidden, her attitude uncertain.

—But I bet she reads me like an open book.
She must have seen my schoolgirl's lead-eyed look

staring back at her a zillion times
while I restructured love's component rhymes.

Tonight's no different. Fingering those seeds
like loose freshwater pearls, or worry beads,

I see pink cosmos whirling on its stem,
and, as if we'd really planted them,

the phlox and midnight-blue lobelia overspill
onto the bed. I'm trying to keep still,

and not to laugh till you're through sketching me —
a charcoal flagrant with expectancy.

## Transmarine

An open hull nudging reeds and sand,
she kept to herself the pleasure he provoked,
the undercurrent dimpling as he stroked,
and drifted, slackly moored under his hand.
Turning to him, she let him loose the knot,
drop the rope, and push his foot against
the pier to lift her free. Her muscles tensed;
he took her like a sail the wind had caught
and guided her until she guided him,
and when they were no place that either knew,
where sky and sea and shadow echoed blue,
they plunged — and were knocked back at the world's rim.

## In Memoriam:
### Franklin Walker III
#### 1954–1988

1.

Some days you slept through my visit,
your eyes not quite closed, but your breath
even. Leafing through *Vanity Fair,*
or *Spy,* whichever you'd requested,
I'd squirm in the squeaky leatherette chair
and finally sleep if I wasn't rested,
my legs stretched out and my feet tucked
between your mattress and the bed guard.
Sometimes you'd sort mail while we talked,
sitting up, knees sharply bent,
checkbook sliding down your thighs,
another well-meant get well card
splayed open and pitched like a tent
on the foothills of your sloping sheets.
One time, when Bunny brought you sweets —
imported, creamy, wrapped in foil
and eagerly devoured — I shrank
to see the empty box on show,
as if it were dark chocolates, Frank,
that made your T-cell count drop low.
Somehow I thought it more loyal
to frown on what you shouldn't eat
and cook brown rice with miso soup
(a Jewish daughter's chicken broth),
as if the food you wouldn't eat
could make you strong. To think of it.

To think how I used to criticize
most what I loved, the extravagant cloth
and substance of your obdurate self,
the cashmeres, leathers, silks, all stuff
both of us prized and coveted,
which you admitted and I did not.
Lanky in your hospital gown,
your high black cheekbones hollowing,
the IV's curling tendril dug
like a thorn into your wrist, your nails
turned black and ridged from AZT,
you wondered how the odds broke down—
would they invent a miracle drug?
Would you survive past thirty-three?

2.
Your patients think you have a cold;
you keep appointments on the phone.
Your parents think you're out of town.
Only closest friends are told.

Potted plants, fresh cut flowers,
friends who call from overseas,
and friends who visit at all hours
lift your spirits by degrees.

Both men and women nurses flirt
because you're sweet as columbine.
Outside your room's a "Danger" sign:
*contagions present; red alert.*

Needles go down a special slot.
Linens into a covered bin.
Across the way, doves in a dovecote
burble and coo, as you grow thin.

Blue masks protect you from our breath.
The staff's equipped with rubber gloves.
It's part of life, outwitting death.
The columbine's named after doves.

A dovecote is a columbary.
A columbarium's a shrine.
You grow more skeletal and weary
until your skin begins to shine.


3.
One afternoon I took a cab
from Mount Sinai to a psychic on Fourth.
We inched through midtown rain and traffic,
zigzagging between lanes, edging
forward sideways like a crab.
Blocking jaywalkers near St. Mark's,
the driver, clearly psychopathic,
warned me away from weirdos, punks,
and other vermin I might meet.
Then he sped up and lurched to hit
every pothole in the street.
Below his rearview mirror, dice
entangled rosary and cross.
I thanked him for the free advice
and rummaged in my purse for change
though thinking only of the loss

to me if you should up and die.
He must have thought my drawn look strange.

The front room was an unkempt shop—
boxes of dusty crystal points
stacked on milk crates against one wall;
the glass display case countertop
crammed with bowls of tumbled quartz,
amethyst eggs, and tigereye.
I looked at chips of opal, jade,
a garnet in its granite matrix,
emerald, turquoise, aquamarine.
Polished amber, light as a leaf,
warmed my open hand. A ball
of deep blue gold-flecked lapis spun
a double helix up my spine—
or was it just the shivers when
I heard distinct derisive snorts
and someone tapped me from behind?
It was a balding snub-nosed man.
He led me into an inner room.

Jeweler's scales stood on the desk.
Bottles of tincture lined the shelves.
He said to sit, to close my eyes,
align my higher and lower selves.
Looking past me to read my aura,
he accessed the Akashic Records
(a kind of karmic accounting book),
flipping through pages in his mind
with fervor, like a student of Torah.
I blurted out your name to ask

the fates how I could help you live.
He cut me off with a look:
"His eyes won't close until he's died.
You're neither mother nor lover, although
in a past life he was your son.
It's not your place to be his guide."
It startled me he mentioned your eyes,
as if that was too much to know.

Too much for me to know. Too much
while you still live to think of death
as your new friend, the rest of us
forgotten. "Fake it till you make it,"
you would say. So I try
to picture you, your red bow tie,
your quick uptake no one can touch;
the way your arm circled my waist;
the time we rode an all-night bus,
and how, that once, we kissed. I play
the years backward till we meet.
The cafeteria. Noon. You've just
woken. Your roommate's girlfriend waves
and introduces us. I taste
it all again and let the years
build up with visits back and forth
till we both live in the city and
I'm standing on the street in tears.

4.
A yellow shaft of light
hovers above your bed.
You watch it with delight.

The dust motes swirl and dance.
Your rapt dreamy look
catches me off-balance.

Standing near your bed,
I'm talking on the phone,
not hearing what is said.

I watch you lift your hand
and turn it in the light
as if you hold a strand

of pearls — and now I lose
the phone call's slender thread.
The sun's full on my face.

The caller doesn't pause.
Slowly you move your hand
and with your fingers trace

the sunlight in my hair.
Your palm brushes my cheek.
I say I'll call right back.

Our fingers interlace
and make a latticed sieve
to cup the buoyant air,

scooping light like sand.
Days later you are dead.
The roses for your grave

are yellow like the sun.
Like light, like air, you live.
We drop them one by one.

*from* Chalkmarks
on Stone

## Beads of Rain

Each day I've looked
into the beveled mirror
on this desk, vainly
asking it questions
reflection cannot answer.

Outside, fog and frost
and silver olive leaves.
I can see at most
a half field's depth,
then the trees are lost
in the gauzy mist
like thin unbraceleted arms
swallowed by billowing sleeves.

I'd like to face
that stringent looking glass
transparent to myself
as beads of rain
pooled on a green leaf.

But ever self-composed
in self-regard,
and my eyes opaque
as a dancer's leotard,
to see straight through myself
I need what love supplies:
its dark arrows, dear,
not its white lies.

## The Trout

Under the hymnal
drone of water
that would drown a shout
I hear you say,
your voice a whisper,
"Come see the trout."
We are down at the kill.

Loose threads of foam
spin out and drift
in the shoal of calm
where you dip your hand
widening a rift
in the light's frayed band
with your open palm.

Glistening, mottled,
mother-of-pearl,
slippery as thought,
it leaps your grasp.
A glide and a swirl:
it's under a ledge
where it can't be caught.

"Give it your pledge
you won't kill it,"
I say, and you swear
you intend no harm,
your voice foursquare
while your fingers flit
from your dangling arm.

Testing your word,
or trusting your voice,
or hearing in it
the soft command
that leaves no choice,
like me, the trout's lured
to feed from your hand.

## Summer Sublet

Sunlight sharp enough to slice
black-eyed susans from their stems,
to sliver stone, so that a wall,
unmortared, laid with river rock
and slab, shimmers in the heat.

Once inside, the flagstone chills
like a gin and tonic, like when
you chew the cubes and I shiver.
At noon, it's too dark to read a book
without a lamp, too dark to tell

the scalloped tin retablo of Mary
that leans on the fireplace mantel
from Grandma's hand-colored tintypes
taken and saved from the shtetl.
I lie on my side on the bed and read,

or else sit at the all-purpose table,
make phone calls, look out the window.
"One day at a time," a neighbor's car,
parked on the narrow washboard road,
reminds me. "One day at a time."

Last week, while I watched him loop
a ristra, red electric chiles, from his door,
he told me that in Asia he strung
electronics, a civilian during war,
then showed me a sunken back room

in his landlord's house, its windows
strafed — a previous tenant's debt.
Testing a warped board with my toe,
I saw my hot plate, desk, and shelves,
before coming to and saying *no*.

New York's as far as Kiev, except
I call, except, like Katmandu,
this is a place the world treks through.
If a sublet's a house of ghosts,
at least they're mostly not ours:

not the broken violin, the Anasazi
shards, the tongue-depressor cross,
not the freezer full of bread and bones.
While sunset pours out drinks pungent
and sweet from the picture window's

chipped pitcher — a peach margarita,
a daiquiri with lime — stacks of postcards
with love from people we haven't met
lean against books we've never read
collecting dust we'll never dust.

Face-up on the half-made bed,
we let summer have its way with us.
When July breaks on our windowsill,
we're awash in its salty marinade
till August sears us on the grill.

## Chalkmarks on Stone

1.

I let the thermometer slide into place,
and think of Persephone waiting for Dis
to tuck another seed under her tongue.
Her mother's daughter, her own mistress,
from the first implacable thrust she was his.
She tallies their days with chalkmarks on stone.
Circles ring those days they make love.
Anticipation's a form of bliss,
her face tilting up like a baby bird's.
Red seed, red juice, raw mouths, red kiss:
a new row, the first marks tinged with blood.
She sees that time comes down to this —
endless cycles scratched in stone
that chronicle her barrenness.

2.

The best of Hades' healers and
the worst line up to treat the Queen
of the Dead behind her lacquered screen.
Some take her pulse; some hold her hand.
One reads the iris of her eye
and gives her drops to feed her blood.
One recommends she bathe in mud.
One flushes out her womb with dye.
Daydreaming over her birth chart,
she looks for clues to "if" and "when."
She breathes in hope like oxygen,
then holds her breath so the tears won't start.

### 3.

Not for all the jewels in her tears,
the sapphires, flawless diamonds, pearls
she so unstintingly pours forth,
would he, by any sign, imperil
his standing as a god, his self-worth,
and let her know how these last years
unmanned him, made him greedy as a child
who's fed, but grabs at any teat,
wailing for his mother's milk.
He keeps Hades' coffers stockpiled,
but it's not for Dis to count his gold.
Her long hair's gold, soft as corn silk.
She sleeps while he untangles it.
Such things can't be bought or sold.
Such things are easily defiled.
He chokes, fighting down self-wrath.
She wakes to an avalanche of tears,
his tears, the minerals for their bath.

4.

Grass, pine, the dangling willow shoots,
elm and aspen leaves in bud,
her mother's softest rumpled sheets,
her chaste luxurious unmade bed,
the scattered sprouts of crocus — all
the earth done up in gorgeous green,
curtained and carpeted for her arrival,
months before fields turn to grain,
with time to bask in the strong light
of her mother's solar-paneled house,
eating her fruits, happy to let
the sun burn off last winter's haze.

5.

She knows the dead, knows how they toil
in furnaces, quarries, mines that yield
a flinty harvest beneath the subsoil.
She's seen them let salt run through their hands,
the way they once had sifted through grain.
But where are the unborn concealed?
Night after restless night, search beams
blaze a dead-end trail through lands
whose border guards patrol her dreams.
Though once, awake, she thought she saw—
unsteady as two newborn fawns—
her children standing in the rain,
waiting for her to come and draw
them in. She reached, and they were gone.

6.

Mornings, in the garden, pulling weeds,
or walking by fields of purple loosestrife,
Persephone thinks back to when,
in love, not caring what would happen,
laughing, she opened her mouth to Dis
to taste his pomegranate seeds
for the first time. Both sweet and tart,
they readied her to be his wife.
She bends to gather fruit that's fallen
ripened in her mother's lap.
Grapes are browning on the trellis.
She'll be home before the cold snap.
Each year her mother says she won't part
with her; each year she lets her go.
Dressed in autumn's cooling mist,
she carries home a handful of pollen
culled last spring from the wild meadow
where he first caught her by the wrist.

## After a Long Journey
### for M. E.

Now you've ridden both elephant and camel;
now you've worn the sackcloth of remorse,

carried the assassin's sap-sticky blade,
the suppliant's lamp of sesame oil, and now

you've planted the warrior's leaf-tipped spear
in front of my mud-hut, reclaiming your stake

in my yes and my no. The gong rings out your hour,
hour and gong both forged in a bellows-fed flame;

your forehead's three forked veins, a trident
throbbing as you stoke the coral bed of coals.

## At the Market Stall

Counting out syllables like pinches of spice,
I choked on their dust, left everything unsaid.

The new moon withered in her cup of darkness.

The peacock closed his iridescent eyes,
his green-fringed fan, and walked, stiff-legged, away.

Turquoise and gold gravel, like filings of
an ant hill, like rubble, lie heaped in a tall mound,
cast from a poem's excavated center.

The node of no: lodged in my throat, a leafless
varnished stump; inexorable seal and stopper.

Then winter's clear acoustics, the pale sun's
slow recuperation; and this, which is mine.

# Relict

The tree itself,
being forbidden,
creates disequilibrium:

in Eden,
as at home,
I'm sure the fruit
looked very sweet
while still on the branch,

like the fresh smell
of unlit tobacco,
like a man not yet kissed.

Relict, he said.
Vestigial.
The heart of the old forest,
the only patch
of these feelings I have left.

Unused to the timbre
of his voice,
across the restaurant table

I stroked his arm,
the new word so delicious,
and the bone of his wrist.

While in Eden,
there was no end
to Eden, you could walk
for years, and never cross
a border, never trespass.

But now, there is
no garden, only this fruit,
still left to eat.

## from *Eclipse*

Handblown vials of Italian inks.
*Oca, rosa, verde, viola.*

A cigar box of letters.
A dozen different addresses.

Three pair of gold hoops.
Innumerable hopes.

The uncut pages of unwritten books.
Reams of rhymes.

A twenty-year's hoard of browning roses clipped
and poured like Chianti into a litre carafe —

spilled out and crushed, to scent this cenotaph.

## Initials

Not carved into the living tree,
but set in concrete
where a dead branch in the crotch
of the trunk had been sawn off—
our initials, still paired and couched
in the flare-backed love seat
of a stick-drawn heart.

I see it every time
I drive in, coming home, next to
the absence of his truck.

I suppose that apple tree
will blossom this spring as always,
first with pink-tinged buds
and then, shiny green leaves.

I suppose by the time the apples
have fallen, I'll be crouched
on my knees, wielding my garden spade
like a palette knife
to spackle over the rough-hewn lines
until that heart and all it encloses
are imperceptible to hand and eye,
like an underpainting,
which keeps on existing, hidden
and contained by whatever is to come.

# Drumming for the Matryoshka

Five-year-old Isabel's
brought her nested dolls,

a brightly shellacked, wooden,
stoic Russian woman

that with a little twist
unscrews at the waist

and once divided in half
reveals another self

cupped inside the first,
the same color as borscht.

Only the smallest one,
the one they radiate from,

cannot be twisted apart.
*She* must be the heart.

While Isabel plays hide and seek,
her mother and I try to talk,

though it doesn't really work.
She wants to play "Joan of the Ark,"

and line us up by twos,
but there's only two of us

and we refuse. What's next?
Her patience is overtaxed.

We've talked enough for one day.
There's other things to do.

The dolls need to wake up.
She shakes the one in her lap,

the one that doesn't unscrew,
small as my big toe.

The rest are scattered around.
She waves a majestic hand,

indicating the homes
of the various *grandes dames:*

one lives inside a saucer;
one's perched atop the toaster;

one's curled up with the cat,
unscratched, but glistening wet.

"We *must* drum them awake!"
She's sizing up the wok,

and clutching a wooden spoon.
We make a great big din,

rattling the china saucer.
Something falls off the toaster.

The cat's out the door.
"More! More! More!"

Isabel's ecstatic.
Her mother looks at the clock

and begins picking up
with a very decisive step.

The Matryoshka are put back together,
one inside the other,

closed with a final twist,
and hugged to Isabel's breast.

We hug each other in turn,
and then, like that, they're gone.

## The Peony

A man cups his fingers as if to bring them
to his lips to blow me a goodbye kiss,
or, as if he were Italian, to underscore
his words. He is not Italian; he is not
speaking; and he does not bring his fingers
to his lips. Gravely, they descend upon a peony
held up by the rim of its fishbowl vase.
Because I would be his, he tells me a secret
it is mine to know, all the while spreading
the silky petals with his slowly opening hand
so that the peony is made to bloom to its fullest,
until it is an open globe, overbrimming the vase.
Only now do I think of those paper flowers
that blossomed when we floated them in water,
as girls. The words of the secret blurred
as soon as I woke, but his light hand
gravely forcing the peony, *that* remains.

## Lines Begun on Yom Kippur
### for Yehudis Fishman

1.
I picture you in a phone booth
as you say your mid-day prayer,
the receiver a prop in your hand.

No one pays any attention
except God, who accepts all charges,
always pleased to be called.

Now, picture me in full lotus,
amid a mandala of crystals,
in front of a burning candle.

If, as you say, this —
our earth — is God's basement,
then that explains the clutter

of co-existence, the profusion
of road maps, the pamphlets
and mislabeled boxes, but why

is it some of us rummage madly
while others sort through one crate
with infinitesimal care?

2.

In that room, I followed Inanna down
and hung by my toes from a thorn tree;

I lay on my back watching the stars
inside the dome of my mother's womb;

I pulled at the gold and silver threads
in her green sari until they snapped;

I followed the dissolving clouds of my breath
but soon they amassed and darkened;

I lay drenched and stunned in that downpour;
I was pelted by stones yanked from my own pocket;

I left myself to die.
I walked to the window.

In a building across the way,
I saw some old men praying at Shul.

They were wearing skullcaps and tallisim.
Each held a prayer book to his breast.

I watched through my curtain while they davened,
bobbing and swaying to greet the Sabbath Queen.

3.

You taught me that the word, in Hebrew,
generates and, by its emanations,
keeps the world in existence;
that each verse in the Book of Lamentations
begins with a different letter,
so that there is an end to suffering.

You said the high should reach down
to elevate the low; that before the Fall,
Adam and Eve had bodies of light,
and, had they waited for the Sabbath,
sanctified, they could have had their fruit.
You said that nothing's so holy and open

as the open rift in a broken heart;
that miracle is catastrophe's correlative.
You said sleep contains a 60th, 'a touch,'
of death; Torah, a touch of Heaven;
Sabbath, Paradise; and dreams, prophecy.
As for poetry . . . that, you've left up to me.

4.

To hear the long and short piercing blasts
of the shofar, I sneaked into a synagogue
a few blocks from my house one Rosh Hashanah.
The service was almost over, so I slipped past
the men in dark suits that guard both doors,
as if I'd just been out stretching my legs.
I was wearing a dress my mother would approve of,
and I found an empty seat right on the aisle.
I even thought of joining that congregation,
but to me, the rabbi in his tall furred hat,
his white embroidered fur-trimmed flowing robe,
looked more like some kind of priest than a rabbi.
Could I, over time, have made up the censer and smoke
that seems closer in spirit to the Holy Ghost
than to the ghastly fumes from the Holocaust?
The cantor's voice filled out the airy dome.
I heard the longed-for sweet and raspy blasts,
then took a walk to the river before going home.

At the river, I leaned over the wooden piling.
Anchor lines clanked against the houseboats and piers.
Pulling some cracker crumbs out of my pocket,
I cupped them against the wind in the palm of my hand.
Like errands, my sins easily slip my mind,
but I compiled a list from the odds and ends
I guessed at or remembered; it was years ago now,
but how much do categories of sins change?
You might lie to yourself one year, your spouse another;
have greed for money, power, greed for fame;
be vain about looks, or just be generally vain . . . .

Gossiping's like a cold that runs its course,
no matter how you try to avoid it. Like envy,
it's hard to shake, but that year, I remember,
I took envy by its anorexic waist
and threw it into the river and watched it drown,
though the crumbs themselves floated in a cluster,
unspiraling as the current sped them away.

## Bosque del Apache

Winter. Scratchy branches flame
upward, stiff as ratted hair.
Crows crown the leafless trees—
black buds that bloom in unison
only to fly. At dawn, the marsh
is crowded as a skating rink;
ducks land in squadrons, swim
in pairs. Geese honk to be let by.
Like them, we're stalled in traffic,
caught in a cavalcade circling
the one-way fifteen mile tour loop,
binoculars in every lap.
We scout to see what we're missing,
and end by missing what we're seeing.
The sky's too busy and too vast.
Lavender-orange masses of clouds,
lit from below, stagily surge
and disperse, while from the farthest East
daylight's dark stars flap their wings,
assume their shifting constellations,
and stream over us, crossing the sky
like corps de ballet after corps de ballet,
undulant velvet ribbons trailing.
Each bird, a basted stitch puckering
the sky's pale blue satin smock;
each flock, an intricate design
in thread the seamstress forgot to lick
and double-knot. And so it goes.
A *V* of cranes unravels, rivaling
the geese for noise.

## Winged Victory

The motel, with its "pay per view,"
is more scenic than the scenic drive
and more exotic, with you
putting your forehead to mine
to check for fever, prescribing cola,
and charting our road, first with one finger,
then your whole hand. . . .

The next day it's tempting to touch
the cavern walls, but we don't,
knowing the oils we secrete
indelibly mar and stain.
Those draperies and columns, thrones
and soda straws — I'd like to see
the Winged Victory among *them*,

not to compare and choose,
but to be doubly bowled over.
The Winged Victory, and what's left
of the Parthenon! But then,
when they turned out the lights
down there, eight hundred feet down,
and it was absolutely unlit,

pitch black, and for a moment
they had us hushed (until someone,
a crying child, broke the silence
and everyone began making noise),
wasn't that hair of a second in total
quiet and darkness, though fleeting,
one of the best moments yet?

That, and the amphitheater at dusk,
watching the cave's long exhalation
of bats, and then the first stars.
The world has so many ways to woo us,
so many unexpected vistas,
and miraculously so much of it (your face
at rest, eyeglasses off ) near at hand.

## Apple Blossoms

To follow the arc of the Big Dipper
as it leads to Arcturus, first I follow the arc

of your arm. In the sand at our feet, the stinkbug's
curved track, each step pronged and linked like vertebrae.

A snake spine could have left the same imprint,
but not a living snake. Rolling down the dune,

we spun together in one cocoon; at bottom,
splayed open, I surrendered to where I fell,

like a cart of apple blossoms overturned at the foot
of your bed. You say to use anything, *anything.*

Like the angels children flapping their skeletal wings
stamp in snow, the angels we made in sand.

## The Butterfly

> "The eye follows the hand
> the mind follows the eye
> the heart follows the mind."
> —from the *Natya Shastra*

With no appreciable weight,
a butterfly alit

and rode my finger
an hour or longer.

Holding my hand ahead,
I let the butterfly lead.

We walked down to the kill,
its wings an upright sail.

I was almost afraid to breathe,
but my feet knew the path—

its slipknot roots
and slingshot branches.

I sat down on a rock.
I couldn't believe my luck.

The world then seemed kind,
a butterfly on my hand,

its bronze wings spread flat,
pulsing to raise its body heat.

Like a fluttering eyelash,
it tickled the web of flesh

between forefinger and thumb.
"My life can never be the same!"

I thought, studying the leopard spots
of its eyes; its veins like pleats;

its scalloped scales; its legs,
six knobby little twigs;

the thorax's fuzzy patina;
the two slender antennae,

bulb-tipped, like matchsticks;
and the pointed black circumflex

markings on each scored wing:
accents from the mother tongue.

With its proboscis it sipped
salt from my hand and tapped

out a secret code,
the secret names of God,

invisible to man,
imprinted on my skin.

If I could have become a fern —
a stone — a stalk of corn . . .

Instead, my left hand twitched
and the butterfly detached

itself, all in a breath,
my article of faith,

momentarily tame
as if out of a dream,

now circling the rock,
not coming back.

*from* **Another Part of the Field**

I count my breath backwards
and forwards; I lift my spine.
At the crown of my head a nest
wobbles. The silver eggs
race round and round the rim
until I lift them out.


Pointing every which way,
the static compass rose,
composed of thirty-two
scrolled and petaled points,
leads nowhere — but divides
the conquered world again.


Taking a walk last week
on a path just off the road,
I saw a camisole,
lavender laced with black,
hanging from a piñon,
just four wheeler height.

Last night the last battered
leaves came flying down, wan
flags drained in surrender.
This morning, the trees are bare,
bereft, like monuments stripped
of gold, like cities plundered.


I heard the blunt thunder,
saw the jagged crossed swords.
My neighbor's horse struck dead
in the arroyo, too heavy to move.
Ribs clean as deer antlers,
skin rough and worn burlap.


It's strange to look inside
and find one's heart a crater,
a moonscape steaming hot
and cold at the same time,
trampled and scarred by what
meteors, whose feet?

It was his *voice,* soft growl
and grit of tenderness,
hypnotic timbre; the way
he checked to see was I
still there, the way his words
like cairns marked out the path.


Today it is a reserve
of love that keeps us tactful-
ly apart: each other's choice,
affection reaffirms
most days—today our vows
in silence best are kept.


The bough shakes in the wind.
Dry leaves rattle down.
Soon the branch is bare,
shocking naked beauty.
When the wind comes up again,
will it also strip my heart?

Connected by a hoof-
worn trail, mountains stand back
to back, imposing bulwarks.
The first I take to be
the highest, but the next
and next loom higher still.


When heaven and earth met
in the first thunder squall,
it took deft hands to plait
the tangled silken threads
of otherworldly weeds
into the rainbow's bridge.


One day, from the ridge top,
scanning Los Alamos,
the Jemez, billboards, our house,
I felt spied on myself,
and turned in time to meet
a coyote's intenser gaze.

This morning we woke to rain.
Scratchy and faint, a dream
came over me in waves—
a late-breaking bulletin—
my sleep's last transmission
before signing off for the day.


After twenty years,
our last talk barely cordial,
over lunch he hands me
a carefully preserved
and love-washed portrait of
myself at seventeen.


We wore black leotards
and snake bracelets; at lunch
we smoked hashish on the lawn.
We knew the word *Rorschach,*
analyzed the clouds,
xeroxed each other's feet.

"Don't hide under a bushel!"—
a distant relative snapped,
going through the sales rack,
a vinyl mini-skirt
and red angora sweater
held out for me to try.


The crab apple outside
our kitchen was just beginning
to blossom the day I left;
the pale pink buds opening,
but not yet open. Now,
home, the grass flecked pink.


Spring, and the kitten wakes
at dawn, mewing at the door—
best to get it done with
and let him out so I
can sleep. Through half-shut eyes,
a glimpse of the white half-moon.

At the entrance to the arroyo,
we walked around the lamb,
its rib cage open and empty,
its wool, like cottonwood snow,
in drifts on the scabbed ground,
coyote scat nearby.

To reach down far enough
into myself to haul up
words pure and cool as water—
I can't seem to. The rope
isn't long enough, or
the bucket's sprung a leak.

Another part of the field.
Another herd of cows.
Someone else's ax
to grind before I chop
and stack his cord of wood,
before his barn's my bed.

Today we saw the hills
of Burma and Laos across
the Mekong; through thin mist:
the Golden Triangle.
Unable to cross the border,
we wet our hands and feet.


Through the window, rice fields
blur the miles, while palm trees
stamp them, and Brahman cows,
girls in school skirts, houses
built on stilts — until
my passport's slid back full.


"Can you see the body?"
He prodded me nearer the pyre
and I saw a charred foot fall
as a cigarette got lit
off a splinter of kindling
laughingly held in the flame.

A mosquito whined in my ear;
a child cried once, and one
rooster crowed, setting off
his minions, thousands of dogs
who barked at the heels of dreams
scurrying home for dawn.


As if between here and there
Scylla and Charybdis,
in wait for my poor ship,
crouch in a narrow strait
like muggers in an alley—
I dread the long way home.


I see them at airports,
bald-headed boys, younger
each year; triangle caps
tucked into their belt loops,
their combat boots oddly
quiet on ramps and stairs.

Were you the cat in the jaws
of the chow Renata found,
poor thing, one paw chomped off,
all rolled in mud, now buried?
Brave Puck, short life of scrapes,
once pillowed by my hair.


Merciless August highlights
the split in our bed's grain,
as if to re-ignite
resentments left from when
it was our battlefield.
The much-rubbed wound shines.


Wind crinkles up the water
like a rippling cloth.
Gently stirred, miso
dissolves in the simmering broth.
I let go of something
I don't name—it's gone.

Whittled down to nothing,
the moon blacks out, spins off,
comes to in a day or so,
sharp as a honed scythe
while the stars dizzily swarm,
bees following their queen.

And now the arroyo's dry wash,
the shifting ridge of hills,
are wave and ocean bed
to me. The juniper,
crenellated coral,
a shell, the shard in my hand.

1992—1994

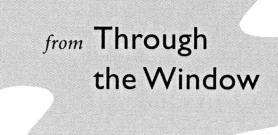

*from* **Through the Window**

Piano music drifts
through the window
and stops. Someone's
composing — a man
with luxuriant Persian hair,
eyes like unmatched stones
set as a close pair.
Leaning on my elbow,
like Rembrandt's Saskia
at her upper story window,
I'll whisper
to no one — not
even him — this reverie.

It's like I'm nineteen—
or sixteen: falling in love,
or drowning in the riptide-pull
of hormones, I'm not sure which.
Like then, interminably confused.
But now I know to read Sappho
and know my passion's nothing
unprecedented, only—unbearable,
always, this longing.
Dumbfounded, ecstatic,
my heart beats breakneck
to hear its torment
so exquisitely laid out.

All night
our two animals
prowl the inner extremities
of their separate cages.
All night
my cat yowls.
Stroking won't subdue her;
her empty maw
stretches wide,
as if . . . as if he's
free to come to her,
as if they still lived
in the woods.

First these poems implore
I write them, pester,
won't stop at no.
Then they betray me,
braying my secrets
to all comers.
It's like planting a rose
for the thorns.

Letters—forbidden.
To see you—
out of the question.
Perhaps I'll write
that book you want,
the one we
talked so much about.

These line ends:
my fingertips
trailing the cleft
of your chin.

Vehement, your voice ragged
and charged, charred by the flame
of unspent desire:
"You're not mine and I'm
not yours!" Had I presumed?
Or were you spooked by your own thoughts,
like a dog barking at his reflection?
I couldn't deny what you'd said,
but inside I did deny it,
I did, I did, I did, I do.

Today I don't feel like I fell in love.
Today I feel it's
all a kind of fever,
a tantric spell, spontaneous combustion,
poetic frenzy, self-immolation,
a sacrifice to the gods
of all I hold dear. Today
I don't feel the ice floe
at the center of my life, I think
I made it up, the way I made up you.

To never let you know.
To never know.

To share only
this poem-bed.

"Stop blaming the poems!"
My muse's voice was stern,
and full of warning.
"It's not their fault
your heart's macheteed in two
and dug out like a cantaloupe,
like a Polynesian canoe.
They might appear to write themselves,
but never have they led you
where you were not already headed.
Their seeds are bedded
in fibre and pulp, mush
of that ripe melon.
Eat or let it rot!"

And you, who've never seen a falling star,
what will you wish on, and what will you wish?

Here, where I am, the stars rub shoulders,
showering me with sparks.

What can I offer you?
I've offered everything to Aphrodite.

Still, there are things I'd like to show you,
things not yet in any poem.

Apache plumes and river clay.
Things in my heart.

The leash is broken.
I'm free, but not unencumbered.

My heart is laden with roses
and pricked by a thousand thorns.

There are so many things to wish for
and so many ways . . .

Let me pull at the roots
of your fine head of hair;

Let me dance a rumba
while you watch.

How simple, if it were just about bodies,
and not about love.

*from* The Lightning Field

## Lou Reed in Istanbul

In the poem I had in mind
one blue-tiled stanza
containing a striped divan
and a single tulip slip
ends at a latticed window

behind whose fretwork
an entire regiment
of red-turbaned tulips
is posted, standing guard
with drawn daggers.

Steam obscured one stanza,
making its marble sweat,
veiling its women's naked
boredom with languor,
their faint mustachios

with clove-scented dew.
(Dew that dissolves
on the tongue like sugar
but tastes bitter-briny,
indigestible as tears.)

A sinuous line of incense
led to an inner courtyard
where someone crouched
over a brass brazier, fanned
wisps of musky smoke

up the bellows of her skirt.
Hearing the click-clack
of my heels on the cobble
she turned to appraise me,
quickly got back to work.

—That mother-of-pearl
intarsiate poem, poem
of the narrow-necked vase,
the bejeweled mirror,
of pumice and water pipes

and plush labyrinthian
women who glide up
from the foot of the bed,
who hide their emotions
"even from the moon"—

Lou Reed shanghaied
that poem, he runs
its arched passageways
despotic as a eunuch,
slouches on its pillows

the sheer-stockinged
corseleted cross-dresser
on *Transformer's* cover
where, in Bilbao at 17,
listening to "Vicious,"

to "Satellite of Love,"
in a Spanish boy's bed
a year before Franco
finally died, high
on codeine cough syrup

I first saw him, his cock
in the facing photo
a concealed nightstick.
Now, listening to his
roughed-up deadpan

under a domed moon
just up the Bosphorus
from Topkapi's seraglio,
watching some starlings
swoop toward the stage

to flit in the lights,
I remember how it felt—
*swoop, swoop, oh baby,*
*rock, rock*—the blood rush
of being set loose.

## Appraisal

Five glass hearts to a hoop.
Chinese coins knotted onto brown silk.
Two sterling silver girls skipping gold wire ropes.

Three emerald beryl beads.
A waterfall of three freshwater pearls.

Angelskin coral cabochons.
Milligrain-edged salmon-colored coral briolettes.

Filligreed dangles.
French screwbacks.

A pair of bezel-set mine-cut diamonds, hinge-hooked.

Her mother's mabé pearls.
Her father's gold-flecked agate eyes.
Sapphires snipped out of a coat's silk lining.

Emerald-cut glass.
A cracked turquoise heart.

Teardrop pearls, off-round to the eye.
One of the sterling silver girls, dew-tarnished.

His angelskin skin.
Her slippery cabochon.

## Conduit

Because the branches of the tall trees surrounding us
are winter bare, the moon has been able to project
its luminance more than usual these past few nights.
I went to bed thinking about the Pashtun word
that translates as "man-with-no-penis" and means
"man-who-doesn't-beat-his wife," but woke up
thinking about a writer I used to know, a woman
whose re-marriage was featured in the Sunday *Times*.
In our courtyard, above the spindle-tip branches,
the moon looked sublime, unfazed by footprints
and flags, the cost of reflecting back to us our secrets
through the one side of its surface ever available
to be read into. Once, on a transatlantic red-eye,
eye level with the moon, I stayed awake all night
leveling with myself, my life stripped clean
under the discipline of her indifferent gaze.
— O Moon, what I want back now is not my naiveté
but my nerve, through which your implacable waves ran.

## Festina Lente

Rake marks on gravel.
Flecks of straw in adobe.

Four and a half feet down,
a blue-glass flask flaking mica,

charred wood, a layer of ash,
a humerus, if not animal,

then human. What looks
like the slatted side of a crate,

the backhoe driver says
is an old well shaft.

Mounds of displaced dirt,
dug up for new leach lines,

rise higher than the walls.
All we know of the pueblo

is that they burned trash here,
in our courtyard; spoke Tewa;

and dispersed—were driven out—
to Santa Clara, to Hopi.

Did the same ditch irrigate
their beans as our flowering plums?

And where we sleep, is that
where their turkeys flocked?

The man who built this house,
scavenging bridge ties for beams,

died in the courtyard,
his sickbed facing sunrise.

His wife's "stitcheries"
still cover some of our windows.

When we reburied the humerus
under a cottonwood, with incense

and a patchwork prayer,
we were only putting it back,

*festina lente,* into the mix
of sieved dirt, sand, and straw.

# The Lightning Field

1.

Four hundred equidistant stainless steel poles,
twenty-five by sixteen, gird and grid the mile-long
kilometer-wide field that was once a plain.
Like polished spears, with solid tapered tips,
they rise over twenty feet. Sounding the air,
attuned to the light's least vibrato,
between dawn and dusk they all but disappear.
It was the hope of lightning drew us here,
and for an hour or so there *is* lightning —
violet strikes, frequent, sharp, and silent
above the mountains ringing the plain
but the poles do not require lightning, they
are aggregate enough. Would we have walked
so casually into the scrub and desert plain
without the reassurance of these metes
and bounds? Past the first gulch, before we reach
the corner pole, the cabin drops below
our line of sight. Quickly, characterize
and distinguish the mountains to the west from the range
to the east. The north. The south. *But we could rely
on the sun,* you say before I've had a chance
to get my bearings, your profile still so new,
studying not the mountains, but the cloud-
lit sky. Leaving the perimeter, we work
our way in, zigzagging from pole to pole.

## 2.

Like an opti-visored basket restorer
interlacing hidden stitches of monocord
to repair a bell-shaped Pomo burden basket,
or like the spider who seemed to be asleep
at the center of a shimmering orb web
that hung by one filament to the bottom knob
of the bronze lantern left of my front door,
until my foot grazed the lower guy wire
and the web collapsed on itself like a string bag,
like a convoluted sentence lacking syntax—
the brain surgeon left signs of his handiwork:
minuscule clips on four arterial walls
and a neatly sutured horseshoe of a scar.
At first, the spider scaled the topmost thread,
retreating to the safety of the lantern,
not so unlike, to the bleeding basket restorer,
the teetering safety of an ambulance
when, last fall, in the middle of the night,
brushing his teeth after a late video
he seized up and fell to the saltillo tile.
Next time I thought to look, the spider, true
to her nature, had rebuilt the radial web.
Just so, they say, will neurons compensate
when some are severed—firing new circuits
across the brain's electrochemical paths.

3.

Although the land itself is rolling and pitted,
the pole-tips form a horizontal plane
flat enough to support a sheet of glass.
Walking among them, you don't notice
the poles' lengths vary by over seven feet—
they look identical; what is disarming
is the languor-inducing rhythm of their recurrence.
They are far enough apart that as you walk
between them it is hard to keep in mind
the multi-angled interrelationships
that subtly tug at you from all directions
when you stop next to any one of them.
Or is it that walking two hundred and twenty feet
(three hundred and eleven, cutting across
the diagonal) allows you to forget?
You might be holding hands, stumbling over
the rough terrain, listening hard for crickets,
absorbed in particular by nothing,
maybe mulling over the near-homonyms
"liar" and "lyre," or talking of love, your love,
and how the breasts on Michaelangelo's women
are like sacs affixed to a man's musculature,
when, mid-sentence, you are stopped up short
by an innocuous-looking juncture, and forced
to scrutinize the meaning of your next step.

4.

Because, as the artist states in his sheet of facts,
"isolation is the essence of land art,"
we were dropped off with two days' worth of food,
having left our car miles behind in Quemado.
Before driving away, the caretaker pointed out
the emergency short-wave radio and assured us
she'd come back to pick us up in forty-eight hours.
Left to ourselves, it didn't take long to discover,
flush with the rough-hewn wall, a secret door,
which, when pushed, sprung open to reveal
mop, bucket, broom, Ajax, and rubber gloves
at the foot of a short set of stairs. These led
to a half attic, too small to stand upright in,
but big enough for the desk and swivel chair
I found — and on that desk, a working phone.
Triumphant as a child who's ferreted out
some slippery unadulterated truth,
I heard the dial tone and ran back down.
But neither of us had any use for my news.
Watching you build a fire in the wood stove,
I rocked in the pine rocker and while we talked
I thought about art's need for subterfuge —
how no construction's straightforward as it seems,
how even the comprehensive-seeming account
of this project's installation omits its cost.

5.

Your mind unkinks itself like carded wool
as one foot steps in front of the other, circling
the five-foot figure-eight infinity loop
painted on tarmac at the beach's edge
in Bolinas. Soon, like a Himalayan ascetic,
you've walked yourself into a waking trance,
not breaking pace for any passerby
who cuts into your path, only asking a man
to move his motorcycle when he begins
to park it where one end of the eight loops back.
You've heard that if a silkworm's cocoon is softened
with water, a continuous thread of silk
will unravel for a thousand yards, and think
the spool a spider draws from must be endlessly
self-renewing, her many spinnerets
producing thread as her design requires.
You keep walking. With each successive loop,
you are being unwound and reconfigured,
a skein of slub silk crisscrossed between thumb
and little finger of an outstretched palm.
Weavers call this bundling a butterfly.
On your way home, a brood of Monarchs hovers
over a field of purple milkweed, roosting.
But one moment you could put your finger on?
There were no omens, only unread signs.

6.

a patch of virga / a verse paragraph
slant marks / slashing the sky / silvered in a shaft
of sunlight / pellucid virgules marking time
and pitch in a run of silent recitativo
no skittering drops / no rivulets of rhyme
shearing off the windshield / dripping from eaves
from leaves / self-contained / this sheet of rain
evaporates / is throttled / bottlenecked
in the sky's throat / never nears / never
grazes / never wets / the tantalized ground
virginal downpour / suspended mid-fall
coitus interruptus / a phone call / a second
thought / a punctured tire / a pummeled breast
no / no / no / no / no
the milk / won't come / the seed / won't plant / the womb
nulliparous / swells anyhow / the rain
falls / and does not fall / stalled / the drops
make no discernible sound / a sob / a soughing
at the wheel / to our right / never overhead
not in reach / always down the road
an etching / scraped / scraped out / scarring the sky
a series of caesuras / a fractured field
a field of splintered bones / of lines broken
into spits smaller than feet / smaller than
a fetus / embryonic / the arrested rain

7.

You could be on a roof hoisting a pipe,
soaking your blistered feet in Epsom salts,
spraying hydrangeas with a garden hose,
ordering pizza, or fiddling with the tiller,
when, before you know it, you've been zapped
by a lightning bolt's millisecond mega-volts.
You might come to curled up in a gravel pit
fifteen feet beyond where you last stood,
your portable radio melted to the spot.
Later you'll say it was like a shot of speed,
or like a bunch of ants running around
inside your body biting. You might have
entrance and exit burns, migraines, nausea,
tingling, blackouts, seizures, kidney damage,
damaged eardrums, sexual dysfunction.
Or like the woman in her son's kitchen
cutting broccoli by an open window,
being struck by lightning could provide
a cure. Though the current knocked her down,
first striking her right foot then traveling up
her leg, up the steel bar implanted when,
a year before, she'd broken her hip in a fall,
when she stood again, a moment later,
her bum leg, which, she said, dragged behind her
"like a sandbag," was completely healed.

8.

I had thought the rectangle of steel shafts
would feel imposed upon the pristine landscape,
an arbitrary postmodern conceit
spoiling the view. But once inside the matrix,
surrounded by the austere expanse, the sleek
sparsely planted forest of tempered poles
fanning out and lofting above me, I found
that the field's exactingly strict geometry
yielded not just jackrabbits, lizards,
blue-winged moths, gilia, and grasshoppers
flinging themselves against my face, but also
a sense of seemingly endless possibility.
Pacing the distance between adjacent poles,
from one vertex to the next we stopped to plot
a makeshift constellation's coordinates,
our footsteps connecting points like dashes to dots
in a child's draw-by-number book of stars.
That no pole stands at the rectangle's center
makes mathematical sense (it's not a square)
but came as a surprise. I'd been keeping count
under my breath, though the farther in we got
the more they blurred together at the far verge.
Midway between the two most central poles
was only a scuffed clod of desert scrub —
an omphalos among the obelisks.

9.

At the center of the world, a seismic hole
cut out of a jade disk inscribed with signs
delicate as a sandpiper's tracks at low tide;
a wrought iron bed in a bare room, a star
of Zion patchwork quilt; your hands, my hips;
falling asleep still joined; every trap
sprung free. Smegma, at the umbilicus,
and bitter ululations for the dead,
love's untranslatable glossolalia
welling up in my throat, tonguing my ear.
Is it a faulty o-ring causes leakage
between worlds, the mystic's watery eye,
the desert altar's perennially trickling spring?
No amount of celestial calculations
can explain that bolt from the blue, that pure
engine of divine kindness that brought us
face to face. At the center of the world,
two molted eagle feathers: one that stands
in a bud vase filled with salt; one held up
by a screw eye. Looking across the room
as caravans of clouds, slow wagon trains,
lumber across the window's quartered plains,
I want to rouse you out of your light sleep,
let you demonstrate, as the clouds drift,
how thoroughly you penetrate my world.

10.

Remember the row of *lux perpetua* candles
lining your bedroom's brick-propped plywood shelf,
each votive wrapped in waxy red-striped paper
stamped with the Virgin's upturned suffering face?
And how, hidden behind the left-hand speaker,
you had a box—no, a *carton* of condoms?
Looking knee to knee at Vermeer's "Lacemaker,"
you showed me how you saw in the loose strands
that overflow the velvet sewing box
an image of the imagination's bounty.
I said that I saw thread, a pair of hands,
a girl's head bent down in taxing concentration,
her own handworked collar framing her face.
I remember you walking backwards into your room,
drawing me with you, toward you, by both hands,
the bundle of fifty yarrow stalks I'd brought
still splayed out on the front room's floor, one stalk
still set apart to stand for the Infinite,
"beginningless beginning and endless end,"
according to the xeroxed instruction sheet.
Not then, not yet, not that first night, but later,
now, I see how liminal and charged
we were in the laced and spiky candlelight,
bending to meet the mattress on the floor,
to meet like changing lines in a full embrace —

11.

Wheelchair to walker to four-prong to cane,
to sometimes, as now, with only the support
of a leg brace, a man (who trekked Nepal
as a teen) works his way back to daydreamed
weekends of catch-and-release fly fishing,
foamy water surging around high boots
that neither leak nor slip. Circling the couch
and coffee table counterclockwise first,
then clockwise, then back, doing an about-face
every few rounds, he tells me as I sit,
my head swiveling, how with a brain injury
like his, affecting the arachnoid membrane,
the farthest points—hands as well as feet—
are last to heal. After a year and a half,
the swath of hair razored out in pre-op
has long been long enough to cover the scar,
but results from recent biofeedback testing
show spatial disorientation, and one hand
hasn't regained its grip—although, he says,
sitting back down, the true imprisonment
doesn't come from the body's limitations,
the most stubborn fucker is still the mind.
"If you look long enough at an abyss
an abyss gazes back at you." His laugh,
always warm and throaty, climbs to a roar.

**12.**

lucid / before the shutter shuts / ox bone
tortoise shell / veins on the back of a hand
lightning's return stroke / a calligraphic
radical / incised in ionized air
abrupt illuminant / shape-shifting glyph
revealing / not what I want / but what *is*
imprinted on the eye / a pseudomorph
ghost weave of disintegrated silk
lozenge-patterned / sawtooth twill / lodged
in the bronze axe / patina it once protected
the fiber purified / the line / distilled
like a thumbprint / secreted in beeswax
a six-week embryo / scanned / on the screen
the ultrasound / grainy as an etch-a-sketch
scanned / then bled out / without / a heartbeat
not "what I want" / but to accept / *what is*
to discern *caul* / from *cowl* / *cowl* / from *shroud*
the unborn / from the dead / grieving from grief
love / help me brush the cinder from my hair
this morning thunder woke me before dawn
patulous with desire / aching to be
part of the rain / pelting the skylight / part
of lightning's jagged latticework / but what
is rain / or lightning / to me / what could I
listening in bed / possibly be / to the rain

13.

The weekend we were at the lightning field
there was no moon. You can't see any lights
from other houses there — there are no houses
(except the caretaker's, which you can't see).
And since there are no highways and no streets —
only the private miles-long dirt road
on which the caretaker drives you in and out —
there are no street and highway lights, no cars,
and no car beams. Also, no town, glimmering
in the distance, no neon casino signs, searchlights,
or brightly lit little league baseball parks.
Once we switched off the few electric lights
inside the cabin, the only source of light
to obscure and/or obliterate the stars
was our flashlight's dim and flickering ray
which you kept trained a foot ahead of our feet,
steering us safely down the kitchen steps
and on for several yards, until the cabin
didn't impede our view of the sky. Then,
like lovers anywhere, the flashlight off,
we stood, eyes closed, and kissed, my back
against your chest, your arms around my waist,
my neck craned back, but not to look, not yet,
at the stars, shifting on their celestial poles,
like voyeurs angling for a better view.

14.

Walking back, as if an axis had gone slack,
we didn't feel that geometric pull
on where we stood and which way we proceeded;
let loose, we were free to cut across the field,
to circumvent the poles, to stop counting.
The meticulously placed prefabricated poles
had come to seem as natural as the cholla
and locoweed the wind sowed here and there.
We barely noticed them, as we wandered out,
we'd grown so used to their enigmatic presence,
and reaching the field's edge we stepped beyond it
without a thought, before we even knew.
Then, on the porch landing, we turned to look.
It must have been the angle of the sun
that made them practically invisible,
consumed by light the way an echo will
consume a sound, and silence consume an echo,
and yet in the air they reverberated still,
a soundless echo of their solid selves,
staves of a faded score — not wholly lost,
not like one of Bach's cantatas being wrapped
around the roots of a transplanted sapling,
or greased and folded up to hold a measure
of grain, the paper scarcer, of more worth
to his widow sold as paper than as song.

15.

Indelible as the potter's smudged thumbprint
on a carbon-dated thousand-year-old shard;
as the silk route traced back to a shred of silk
plaited in an Egyptian mummy's hair;
as a leaf-shaped lime burn scarring a left wrist;
as Cossack hooves heard from inside a cold oven —
while to someone else the rain brings back nights
of caged silkworms chewing on mulberry leaves,
and for me, walking the city's gridded blocks,
tears that didn't fall but never stopped
sounding inside me. Until all at once they did
stop, leaving an exquisite quiet,
and the air clear. As after a lightning storm,
when the sky's electrical balance is restored,
quintillions of electrons having swarmed
earthward, through a channel five times as hot
as the sun. As my friend described the bodiless voice
it could not have been more emphatic or distinct:
"Not one breath, not one heartbeat, is your own."
After that, he never took psilocybin again,
and began keeping his Covenant with God.
Before searching the sky for Hyakutake,
first I trained my binoculars on you.
In the desert, your eyes must be strong as stone.
But come, close them now, rest them in this dark.

16.

Seen from above, I think the lightning field
must look like a bed of nails, or garden spikes,
a force field of ambiguous auspices,
an artifact with calendric implications.
Although an aerial survey did determine
which way the field was positioned on the land,
the artist declares that an aerial view
is of no value — the experience takes place
within the field, walking among the poles,
in a small group, or alone. Set in concrete
foundations one foot down and three feet deep,
each pole — engineered to hold its own
in wind up to one hundred miles per hour
and cut to within an accuracy of one
one-hundredth of an inch to its own length —
is a single line in an abstract poem,
the surface repetition unfathomable
while meaning accrues across the full array
which never can be walked the same way twice.
I *wanted* to retrace our steps, the air
to vibrate with the same electric hum,
unseen cicadas, flashes of forked lightning,
but the terrain shifted under my feet,
and each confluence I thought I recognized
a play of light invariably transformed.

# Geese

We called them ducks, but they were geese, Canadian geese.
When they dipped their beaks into the water to nibble pond-scum
their tails tipped up, and their bodies bobbed, like buoys —
   a row of geese, a string of buoys.

For two weeks we watched them from the windows and deck
of our rented boathouse overlooking the saltwater pond.
Beyond the edge of the pond, which wasn't that far, you could see
   a rocky beach, a strip of sea.

The gestation had just begun. Swimming through moon jellies
and reeds to the middle of the pond, I liked to see how close I could get
to the placidly floating ducks, which is how I thought of the geese.
   Flotilla of ducks, armada of geese.

So as not to disrupt the delicate orchestration going on within,
I swam sidestroke, gliding along the surface of the water like one
of the geese, one of the ducks, my eyes fixed on the shore.
   Idle moorings, the houses on shore.

But each time I swam in the pond, the pond reeds ribboned
and swirled over my thighs, exerting such a gently seductive suction
that I imagined them pulling me down, onto a bed of reeds —
   a sea-creature's lair, the swaying reeds.

And though we were already home by the time the bleeding began,
looking back now I can remember pushing aside what part of me knew
as I looked out the window, weighing my breasts in my hands,
   watching the geese, my breasts in my hands.

## Report

The articulation of my bones
a bird's, I woke not just not knowing
where or who but *what* I was:
my opened arm a wing in which she rested,
the two of us fuscous and fused
in the feathery half-dark
until that consciousness that's always
roving, testing, that's roving now,
striving to assemble an accurate report,
probed further into the feeling
and found me made of string and straw,
bits of silky floss licked together,
a nest shaped to fit her unfledged shape,
an account of ourselves I accepted
until daylight pried apart the louvers
and I discovered myself fingering
the soft stubbles of her shaven hair.

## Birthstone

Each morning I eat an orange
from the bagful given us
by the head of the orphanage
and still the bag is full.

Afternoons on the tour bus
you sit in my lap and sleep
or cling to my garnet necklace
biting it with all four teeth.

Out the bus's window
the bicyclists of Guangzhou
balance boxed refrigerators
and crates of live hens

above their back spokes.
*Look ma, no hands*
another new parent jokes
as he refocuses his lens

to catch a trio of girls
turning perfect cartwheels
before they begin to squeal
and mug for the camera.

A cluster of girls that age
and one albino boy
posed for their pictures
that day at the orphanage.

"Welcome American families"
the chalkboard read.
*These are our best babies*
your father overheard

someone say in Mandarin
as you were carried in
and I shot out of my seat
to take you from your "auntie"

and hold you close.
You were wearing layers
on layers of clothes
topped by bulging overalls

and pink appliquéd
white cotton shoes
too small for your toes
but soft and delicate.

*Yours.* And you *mine.*
Under close-cropped hair
your big eyes took me in
with a glint of recognition.

Then, after an exchange
of currency and gifts,
everyone stood to watch
the new mothers change

their babies' diapers,
the adolescent girls
and one albino boy
just outside the door

looking sweet enough
to forgive the inexplicable,
that none of us had come
to take them home.

*Tug, tug all you like,*
*my darling—tug till you're back*
*asleep, tug in your dreams,*
*start tugging again*

*the minute you wake—*
*no matter how hard*
*you tug, your birthstone*
*necklace will not break.*

## Studies in Pen and Ink

> "Just because a bird flies over
> your head, doesn't mean you have to build
> a nest for it in your hair."
> — Martin Luther

1.
A cigarette tucked at a rakish angle
behind a donkey driver's ear,

a gold coin in the ear's whorl;
a man and a woman bouncing along behind him

in his cart, while a woman in a silk chemise
stands to adjust her garter and black stocking,

one foot up on the cart's nearest wheel,
a man's disjointed arm jutting between her legs,

in his fist a rock, aimed at a rottweiler.
"Krishna" in parentheses— the driver's name.

2.

Taped to a self-portrait:
a news clipping, an AP photograph
of four Croatian soldiers mugging
for the camera, in what was then
Tomislavgrad, Yugoslavia.
The artist looks like herself,
and one of the soldiers looks
like the artist, which must be why
she thought to make the sketch.

Both women's waists are cinched
over bulky camouflage jackets; each
has one foot off the ground,
as if leaping; both smile, dimpled,
exuberant; a pistol handle sticks out
of each one's side pant pocket;
each raises two fingers in a *V*,
but only the real soldier
has nail polish visible on her thumb.

3.
Bite marks on a bent foreknuckle.
Fingers spread to press flat

a poem's crumpled tearsheet.
Wrists at the center of a pinwheel.

Going clockwise, the crosshatched
overlapping sets of hands

are cupped, relaxed, grasping, clenched,
and then—a knotted rheumatoid claw.

Index and middle fingers raised
in a *V*; repeated once, turned

sideways, a pair of scissors
snipping, snipping away at the page.

4.

The man and the woman
whose breast he cups from behind
exist on the same plane,

while the sprawling man
whose hand clutches for her thigh,
and the woman who leans over

the edge of the bed, the man
pursing his lips, the one
kneeling to pray, are drawn

at diagonals and the contact
they make is wayward, tangential.
Her eyes are closed. Her hands

are bound. Her hands are
half-erased. She has more arms
than Vishnu. Arching one

behind her, she encircles
her lover's head, and pressing
the base of his skull,

presses his mouth to her neck.
Hands crumple the bedsheets, open
like a lotus. One covers

the hand at her breast, one's flat
at her side. One's crooked
at the elbow, suppressing a yawn.

5.

The strawberry da Vinci drew in cross-section
on one side of a notebook page bleeds through

to cushion a fetus floating on the back.
By now, the ink has browned, the paper's cracked,

dimly lit, encased upright and displayed
in glass for us to circle, case after case

of notebook pages we pause before and pass
in accelerating knots and curlicues —

*the coition of a hemi-sected man
and woman* no more absurd or accurate

than a flying machine. A tube from the testicles,
*the seat of ardor,* leads straight to the heart.

Once, in a videotape of surgery,
I saw fimbria wafting in the body's fluid

like seaweed under water. The ovaries looked
like sponge or coral. Here, the woman's heart's

a dial. I hear my own timer ticking,
ticking fast, the parts dissected, tagged,

and reassembled, but never yet disarmed.
Or detonated. Here, here's the blueprint,

recto and verso, marked up in mirror script.
The deeper I delve, the more I feel objective.

Pushed by the crowd, we rush through in under an hour:
a living page, one of the studies on water.

6.
Landscape with a corn snake
sunning itself on a husked branch
of a dead tree. Afternoon shade
gloves a left hand. The waterfall's

diaphanous shawl's a yashmak,
leaves only the eyes unveiled—
the third eye, like a horse's blaze
on the stone forehead. Hoofprints

brand the wet grass; the pool's
scattershot with catkins and leaves.
Rock moss oozes between my toes
as I wade in, testing the water,

the watermark, the ink, the line,
the line of argument, the pen.
—And in my hair, a myriad
of nests, one for every bird.

# Notes

p. 15  "Quilted Pantoum" incorporates phrases from Agnes Martin's *Writings* (Ostfildern-Ruit: Cantz Verlag, 1991).

p. 105  The *Natya Shastra* is the ancient Indian treatise on the performing arts.

p. 110  The six-line poems of *Another Part of the Field* were inspired by the hexagrams of the *I Ching*. The stanzaic form derives from the hexagrams' six lines, the 3-beat line from the three coins diviners use to "cast" those lines.

p. 141  The italicized words in the last stanza are from "Andy's Chest" on Lou Reed's 1972 album, *Transformer*.

p. 146  The Lightning Field is a site-specific installation by Walter De Maria outside of Quemado, New Mexico. The information throughout the poem about the lightning poles' arrangement and engineering as well as the artist's intent are taken from the artist's statement, "Some Facts, Notes, Data, Information, Statistics, and Statements," which is available at the field and was published in *Artforum,* XVIII:8 (April 1980).

p. 157  A pseudomorph is a piece of silk whose physical structure survives imprinted on the patina of ancient bronze vessels.

p. 171  The phrases in italics are taken from Leonardo da Vinci's notebooks.

# Acknowledgments

Grateful acknowledgment is made to the editors of the following journals and anthologies in which these poems, sometimes in earlier versions, previously appeared:

AGNI, *Another Desert: Jewish Poets of New Mexico* (Sherman Asher), *Blue Arc West: An Anthology of California Poets* (Tebot Bach), *Blue Mesa Review, The Blue Moon Review, The Carolina Quarterly, Chicago Review, Chokecherries* (SOMOS), *Colorado Review, Conjunctions, Denver Quarterly, The Drunken Boat,* FIELD, *First Intensity, Forward, Harwood Review, Just Outside the Frame: Poets from the Santa Fe Broadside* (Tres Chicas Books), *Looking Back to Place* (Old School Books), *Manoa, New Mexico Poetry Renaissance: A Community on Paper* (Red Crane), *The New Republic, The New Yorker, Noctiluca, The Onset Review, Orion, The Paris Review, Parnassus, Partisan Review, Pinchpenny, The Practice of Peace* (Sherman Asher), *Puerto del Sol, Pushcart Prize XXVI* (Pushcart Press), *River Styx, Solo, So Luminous the Wild Flowers* (Tebot Bach), *Southwest Review,* THE, *The Threepenny Review, Triquarterly, Under 35: The New Generation of American Poets* (Anchor Books), *Volt, Walk on the Wild Side* (Charles Scribner's Sons and Collier Books), *Web Conjunctions, Western Wind: An Introduction to Poetry* (McGraw-Hill), *Wild and Whirling Words* (Etruscan Press).

*Taken from the River* was first published by Alef Books in 1993. *Chalkmarks on Stone* was first published by La Alameda Press in 1998. *Through the Window* was first published in Istanbul by Iyi Seyler in 1988, as *Pencereden/*

*Through the Window,* a bi-lingual edition translated into Turkish by Nezih Onur. A second edition was published by La Alameda Press in 2001. *The Lightning Field* was first published by Oberlin College Press in 2003. I wish to thank my editors — especially Philip Brady, Andrew McCord, Edwin Frank, Jeff Bryan, Martha Collins, David Young, and David Walker — for their support.

In the first section, new poems, sometimes in slightly different form, first appeared in the following publications: *Ars Interpres:* "Matter and Spirit," "Out of the West," "Vapor Trail"; *Chokecherries:* "Out of the West"; *City Art Journal,* "Vapor Trail," "Matter and Spirit"; *Epiphany:* "Narcissi," "Still Life," "Torn Silk," "The Light Out Here"; *FIELD:* "So Late, So Soon," "Ballast," "Bone Soup"; *Harwood Anthology* (Old School Books): "Pantoum Quilted from Agnes Martin's *Writings*"; *Narrative Magazine:* "Every Which Way," "October Sunrise," "Premonition"; *The New Republic:* "Pantoum Quilted from Agnes Martin's *Writings*"; *Platte Valley Review:* "Canning in Chimayo"; *Salamander:* "From the Other Side of the World."

I also wish to thank Jeremy Stone for putting me in touch with the Richard Diebenkorn Foundation, and the Estate of Richard Diebenkorn for granting me permission to reproduce "Large Still Life, 1966."

Finally, I am grateful to the National Endowment for the Arts for a poetry fellowship, the Lannan Foundation for a writer's residency in Marfa, Texas, and the MacDowell Colony and Virginia Center for the Creative Arts for residencies.

# Carol Moldaw

Carol Moldaw was born in Oakland, California. She is the author of a novel, *The Widening,* and four previous books of poetry — *The Lightning Field,* which won the 2002 FIELD Poetry Prize; *Through the Window; Chalkmarks on Stone;* and *Taken from the River.* Her poems have appeared in numerous journals and anthologies, and have been translated into Turkish, Chinese, and Portuguese. She has taught at Stonecoast, The University of Southern Maine's Low-Residency MFA Program; The Naropa University; and The Taos Summer Writers' Conference. The recipient of a Lannan Foundation Marfa Writer's Residency, NEA Creative Writing Fellowship and Pushcart Prize, she lives in Pojoaque, New Mexico, with her husband, Arthur Sze, and their daughter, Sarah.

# Books from Etruscan Press

Founded in 2001 with a generous grant from the Oristaglio
Foundation, Etruscan Press is a non-profit cooperative
of poets and writers working to produce and promote
books that nurture the dialogue among genres, achieve
a distinctive voice, and reshape the literary and cultural
histories of which we are a part.

ETRUSCAN IS PROUD OF SUPPORT RECEIVED FROM
Wilkes University
Youngstown State University
National Endowment for the Arts
North East Ohio MFA program
The Wean Foundation
The Ohio Arts Council
The Stephen & Jeryl Oristaglio Foundation
Nin & James Andrews Foundation
Council of Literary Magazines and Presses
Ruth H. Beecher Foundation
Bates-Manzano Fund
New Mexico Community Foundation

# etruscan press

WWW.ETRUSCANPRESS.ORG

Etruscan Press books may be ordered from

CONSORTIUM BOOK SALES
AND DISTRIBUTION
800.283.3572
www.cbsd.com

SMALL PRESS DISTRIBUTION
800.869.7553
www.spdbooks.com

Etruscan Press is a 501(c)(3) nonprofit organization. Contributions to Etruscan Press are tax deductible as allowed under applicable law.

For more information, a prospectus,or to order one of our titles, contact us at etruscanpress@gmail.com.

Book design is by Arlyn Eve Nathan. The textface used is Minion, designed by Robert Slimbach in 1989. The accompanying titles are set in Gill Sans designed by Eric Gill in 1927. The flourishes are from Bodoni's ornaments.